THE BIG GAME

THE SUMMER OLYMPICS

WORLD'S BEST ATHLETIC COMPETITION

Matt Scheff

Lerner Publications ◆ Minneapolis

Lerner Publications Company
An imprint of Lerner Publishing Group, Inc.
241 First Avenue North
Minneapolis, MN 55401 USA

For reading levels and more information, look up this title at www.lernerbooks.com.

Main body text set in Conduit ITC Std.
Typeface provided by International Typeface Corp.

Editor: Alison Lorenz **Designer:** Viet Chu

Library of Congress Cataloging-in-Publication Data

Names: Scheff, Matt, author.
Title: The summer Olympics : world's best athletic competition / Matt Scheff.
Description: Minneapolis : Lerner Publications, 2021 | Series: The big game (Lerner sports) | Includes bibliographical references and index. | Audience: Ages 7–11 | Audience: Grades 2–3 | Summary: "Explore the excitement of the Summer Olympics through its biggest stars, jaw-dropping feats, and dazzling gold-medal moments. In this behind-the-scenes look, readers learn how the games' great spectacle comes together"— Provided by publisher.
Identifiers: LCCN 2019036651 (print) | LCCN 2019036652 (ebook) | ISBN 9781541597570 (library binding) | ISBN 9781728401256 (ebook)
Subjects: LCSH: Olympics—History—Juvenile literature.
Classification: LCC GV721.5 .S356 2021 (print) | LCC GV721.5 (ebook) | DDC 796.48—dc23

LC record available at https://lccn.loc.gov/2019036651
LC ebook record available at https://lccn.loc.gov/2019036652

Manufactured in the United States of America
1-47861-48301-1/28/2020

Contents

Michael Phelps swims the butterfly stroke at the 2008 Olympic Games.

One Last Surge

Michael Phelps stepped to the starting platform for the 100-meter butterfly final. It had already been an amazing 2008 Summer Olympics for Phelps. But the 100-meter butterfly was his biggest challenge.

Serbian swimmer Milorad Cavic dove into the pool with a perfect start. He pulled ahead of the rest of the field. Phelps pumped his arms, gaining on Cavic. But Cavic held his lead as the swimmers pushed forward. With one final stroke, Phelps surged toward the wall.

Finally, the results appeared on the scoreboard. Phelps had won by 0.01 of a second! Phelps went on to win a record eight medals at the 2008 Olympic Games.

Facts at a Glance

- The Olympics first took place in ancient Greece. After more than a thousand years, French historian Pierre de Coubertin brought them back in 1896.

- Nadia Comaneci scored the first perfect score in Olympic gymnastics in 1976. She went on to earn six more perfect scores in the same Games.

- Michael Phelps has the most medals of any Olympic athlete. He won 28 medals, 23 of which are gold.

- About 3.6 billion people watched at least some of the 2016 Summer Olympics.

Fans wave Greek flags at the 2004 Olympic Games in Athens, Greece.

CHAPTER 1

THE SUMMER GAMES

THE MODERN OLYMPICS TRACE BACK TO ANCIENT GREECE. Athletes tried to run, jump, and wrestle their way to glory. The ancient Games died out in the fourth century. Then, in 1896, French historian and teacher Pierre de Coubertin brought the Olympics back. He saw them as a way to increase international cooperation.

Dark Days and Return

War shut down the Games over the next few decades. The 1916 Olympics were canceled due to World War I (1914–1918). World War II (1939–1945) wiped out the 1940 and 1944 Games.

The Olympics returned in 1948. More than 50 nations came to compete. Soon that rose to 100. As they grew, the Olympics sometimes became political. The Games suffered a terrorist attack in 1972. Through the late 20th century, the Soviet Union—a group of countries that included Russia—and the United States had a fierce Olympic rivalry. Due to political tension, each nation refused to compete in Games hosted by the other.

Athletes pass the Olympic flame at the 1948 Games.

The US sat out the 1980 Games, while the Soviet Union sat out the 1984 Games.

By the 1990s, the focus of the Games had returned to international cooperation. Athletes such as Michael Phelps, Usain Bolt, and Simone Biles became worldwide celebrities. The Games give athletes and fans from around the world the chance to come together. Countries take part in friendly competition and celebrate their love of sports.

Sprinter Florence Griffith Joyner of the United States won five Olympic medals in the 1980s.

Inside the Game

The 1908 Olympics introduced the marathon. The long-distance foot race comes from the Greek legend of Philippides. Legend says the messenger ran from the Battle of Marathon to Athens without stopping. The modern marathon is about 26 miles (42 km).

Jamaica's Usain Bolt sprints in the 100-meter race during the 2008 Olympics.

Jesse Owens (*far right*) crosses the finish line to win the 100-meter race at the 1936 Olympics.

CHAPTER 2

Memorable Moments

THE 1936 GAMES IN BERLIN, GERMANY, WERE TENSE. Many countries worried about Germany's Nazi Party and its leader, Adolf Hitler. The Nazis believed in the superiority of white Germans. They spread a message of hatred for other races.

Athletes of color had to compete in a nation whose leaders saw them as less than human. One athlete, Jesse Owens, was a black track-and-field star from the United States. He won four medals as the crowd cheered him on. Ten black Americans brought medals home. Their victories flew in the face of Nazi Germany's racist policies.

Owens sprints for the finish line.

No Shoes Required

Abebe Bikila of Ethiopia arrived in Rome, Italy, for the 1960 Games. He was a last-minute replacement for an injured marathoner. Bikila had packed a brand-new pair of shoes to wear for his event. But the shoes did not fit him.

Bikila did the only thing he could. Barefoot, he took his place at the starting line and began to run. As other runners tired and slowed, Bikila pulled into the lead. Bikila earned gold, crossing the finish line in 2 hours, 15 minutes, 16 seconds. In 1964, he won the marathon again, this time wearing shoes.

Abebe Bikila (*center*) passes fans on his way to victory in 1960.

Bikila's marathon time set an Olympic record in 1960. At the next Games, he cut it by three minutes!

PERFECT 10

At just 14 years old, Nadia Comaneci competed at the 1976 Games in Montreal, Canada. The young gymnast swung, spun, and soared through the uneven bars competition. Her routine was flawless. But when her score flashed on the scoreboard, it read 1.00, or one point.

Nadia Comaneci performs on the balance beam at the 1976 Olympics.

The scoreboard was not set up to show a score above 9.99. The 1.00 represented a perfect 10.0. Comaneci was the first Olympic gymnast to receive a perfect score. She earned six more on her way to becoming the all-around gold medalist.

Gymnasts need total control to perform moves atop the balance beam.

Inside the Game

A score of 10.0 used to be the highest possible score in gymnastics. That changed in 2006. The new system combines a routine's level of difficulty with how well the athlete performs the moves. Because athletes can always try more difficult moves, the new system has no highest score.

SMASHING RECORDS

US swimmer Katie Ledecky was a star of the 2016 Games. She won five medals, including four golds, as she raced through the pool.

In the 400-meter freestyle finals, Ledecky left the other swimmers in her wake. With powerful strokes and kicks, she surged to the wall as the crowd went wild. Her time of 3:56:46 smashed the world record by two seconds. The next swimmer came in five seconds behind her.

Ledecky celebrates her gold medal win in the 400-meter freestyle.

Ledecky powers through the pool at the 2016 Olympic Games.

Mildred "Babe" Didrikson practices a sprint before her Olympic tryouts in 1932.

CHAPTER 3

CLUTCH PERFORMERS

FANS LOVE TO WATCH THE WORLD'S GREATEST ATHLETES performing at their best. Swimmers glide through the water to set records. Gymnasts soar through the air. Sprinters and long jumpers speed and leap down the track. Read on to learn about some of the greatest Olympic athletes of all time.

Michael Phelps

No athlete has won more Olympic medals than US swimmer Michael Phelps. From 2000 to 2016, Phelps won an amazing 28 medals, including 23 gold. Phelps's biggest moment came in the 2008 Games. He won eight gold medals, the most ever won in a single Olympics. He broke seven world records along the way.

FLORENCE GRIFFITH JOYNER

US sprinter Florence Griffith Joyner won her first Olympic medal in 1984, taking home silver in the 200-meter event. In 1988, Flo-Jo dominated. Griffith Joyner won four more medals, three of them gold. In the 200-meter event, she broke the world record in the semifinals. Then she broke it again in the finals!

USAIN BOLT

Usain Bolt, known to fans as the fastest man alive, sprinted to fame in the 2008 Olympics. He won gold in both the 100-meter and 200-meter events and claimed two world records. Bolt won both events again in 2012 and 2016. He added two gold medals in relay events. Over the three Games, Bolt took home eight Olympic medals, all of them gold.

BABE DIDRIKSON

Babe Didrikson was a triple threat. At the 1932 Games, she won gold in the 80-meter hurdles and the javelin. Then she took silver in the high jump. No other track-and-field athlete has won medals in running, jumping, and throwing events in a single Olympics.

STEVE REDGRAVE

Few Olympic athletes have stayed at the peak of their sport longer than Steve Redgrave did. The British rower won gold medals at five different Olympic Games. His first rowing medal came in 1984. His streak carried through 2000, when he won gold at the age of 38.

LARISA LATYNINA

Larisa Latynina was the greatest gymnast of her time. From 1956 to 1964, she won 18 medals for the Soviet Union. Her medal count was an Olympic record until Michael Phelps beat it in 2012. In 1956, Latynina took home gold medals in the vault, floor exercise, all-around, and team events.

EMIL ZATOPEK

Czech distance runner Emil Zatopek won his first gold medal at the 1948 Olympics. But the 1952 Games made him a legend. Zatopek won the 5,000-meter, 10,000-meter, and marathon events all in the same Games. The marathon was the first Zatopek had ever run.

SIMONE BILES

In 2016, US gymnast Simone Biles earned four individual gold medals. She also led the US team, nicknamed the Final Five, to a gold medal in the team event. In 2019, Biles became the first woman in history to land a triple-double, a floor exercise with two flips and three twists in the air.

Fans cheer at the 2016 Olympic Games in Rio de Janeiro, Brazil.

CHAPTER 4

Olympic Culture

THE SUMMER OLYMPICS IS A HUGE GLOBAL SPECTACLE. Every four years, fans and athletes from around the world travel to a new host city. Each Olympics takes on the flavor of its host city and nation. Fans crowd in to watch achievements on the track, in the pool, and at the gymnastics center. Away from the Games, fans and athletes soak in the local food, music, and architecture.

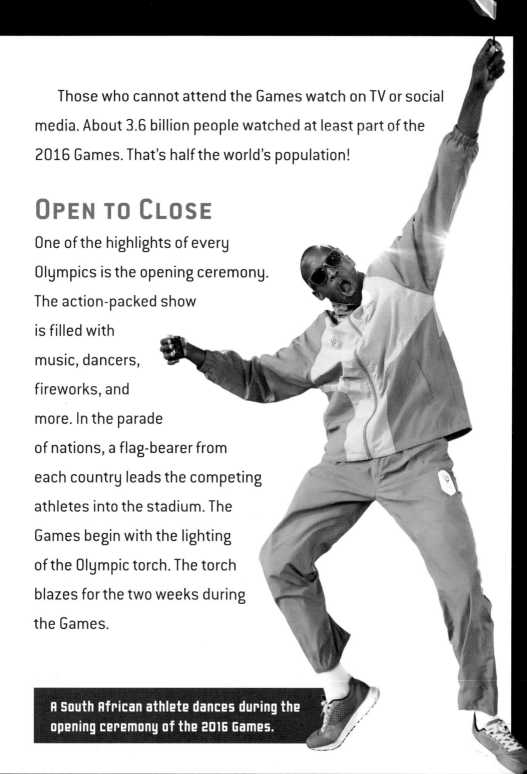

Those who cannot attend the Games watch on TV or social media. About 3.6 billion people watched at least part of the 2016 Games. That's half the world's population!

Open to Close

One of the highlights of every Olympics is the opening ceremony. The action-packed show is filled with music, dancers, fireworks, and more. In the parade of nations, a flag-bearer from each country leads the competing athletes into the stadium. The Games begin with the lighting of the Olympic torch. The torch blazes for the two weeks during the Games.

A South African athlete dances during the opening ceremony of the 2016 Games.

Countries honor winners in medal ceremonies. Athletes stand on podiums to receive their awards. Gold medalists hear their national anthems played. When their events are over, many athletes stay to cheer on the other competitors.

Gymnasts hold up their medals in 2016.

Inside the Game

Many athletes stay in an area called the Olympic Village. It's just for athletes, off-limits to fans and reporters. In the Village, athletes mingle, relax, and prepare for their events. Some make lifelong friends from around the world.

The closing ceremonies end the Games. These celebrations are usually smaller than the opening ceremonies. But for many fans and athletes, they're an important part of concluding the competition.

Meanwhile, preparations for the next Games have already begun. Another host city is getting ready to welcome the world to the biggest sporting event on Earth.

When the 2016 Games came to a close, many athletes were already looking ahead to the 2020 Games in Tokyo, Japan.

THE CHAMPIONS

Which nations won the most medals at each of the Summer Olympic Games? Read on to find out!

Year	Nation	Medals Won
1896	Greece	46
1900	France	100
1904	United States	239
1908	Great Britain	146
1912	Sweden	65
1916	Canceled due to war	
1920	United States	95
1924	United States	99
1928	United States	56
1932	United States	103
1936	Germany	89
1940	Canceled due to war	
1944	Canceled due to war	
1948	United States	84
1952	United States	76
1956	Soviet Union	98

Year	Nation	Medals Won
1960	Soviet Union	103
1964	Soviet Union	96
1968	United States	107
1972	Soviet Union	99
1976	Soviet Union	125
1980	Soviet Union	195
1984	United States	174
1988	Soviet Union	132
1992	Unified Team (former Soviet Union)	112
1996	United States	101
2000	United States	97
2004	United States	101
2008	United States	110
2012	United States	104
2016	United States	121

Glossary

architecture: the art and style of buildings

butterfly: a swimming stroke in which the swimmer uses both arms to move forward

ceremony: a formal, regular series of events

international: involving two or more nations

marathon: a long-distance foot race of 26 miles (42 km)

political: involving government or relationships between different governments

rivalry: intense competition between two players, teams, or nations

spectacle: a large, impressive public display

sprint: to run as quickly as possible, usually for a short distance

vault: a leap in which an athlete uses both hands to push off

Further Information

Ducksters: Ancient Greece: Olympics
https://www.ducksters.com/history/ancient_greek_olympics.php

Gitlin, Marty. *Olympic Track and Field Legends*. Mankato, MN: Black Rabbit Books, 2021.

Lawrence, Blythe. *Behind the Scenes Gymnastics*. Minneapolis: Lerner Publications, 2020.

Olympic Games Facts for Kids
https://kids.kiddle.co/Olympic_Games

Rule, Heather. *Olympic Games Upsets*. Minneapolis: Lerner Publications, 2020.

The Summer Games
https://www.olympic.org/summer-Games

Index

Photo Acknowledgments

Image credits: TIMOTHY CLARY/AFP/Getty Images, p. 4; Hendrik Sulaiman/EyeEm/Getty Images, p. 5; Jonathan Ferrey/Getty Images, p. 6; Topical Press Agency/Getty Images, p. 7; Tony Duffy/Allsport/Getty Images, p. 8; Alexander Hassenstein/Bongarts/Getty Images, p. 9; Keystone/Getty Images, p. 10; Getty Images, p. 11; AFP/Getty Images, p. 12; Keystone-France/Gamma-Keystone/Getty Images, pp. 13, 22 (lower); Mondadori Portfolio/Getty Images, p. 14; The Asahi Shimbun/Getty Images, pp. 15, 22 (upper); Ryan Pierse/Getty Images, p. 16; Adam Pretty/Getty Images, pp. 17, 19; Bettmann/Getty Images, pp. 18, 21 (upper); Mike Powell/Allsport/Getty Images, p. 20 (upper); Shaun Botterill/Getty Images, p. 20 (lower); Professional Sport/Getty Images, p. 21 (lower); Laurence Griffiths/Getty Images, p. 23; TASSO MARCELO/AFP/Getty Images, p. 24; Cameron Spencer/Getty Images, p. 25; Stanislav Krasilnikov/Getty Images, p. 26; Pascal Le Segretain/Getty Images, p. 27; Mark Sagliocco/Getty Images, p. 28. Design elements: Tuomas Lehtinen/Getty Images; zhengshun tang/Getty Images. Cover image: Alex Livesey/Stringer/Getty Images.